The Perfection
Of
Purity

By: Patrick Baldwin

Table of Contents

Invitation

Please Scroll to the Back of the Book for

A Special Gift from God

If You Would Like to Share Your Story with Us or Stay in Contact Our Contact Information Can Be Found in the Back of the Book As Well

Remember . . . .

~God Is Able~
Regardless of the Situation

Dedication

This Book is Dedicated to My Daughter with Love

You have forever changed My Heart – I hope to Guide Yours Now As You Consider Your Future Husband and Family to Come

-You Will Always Be My BB-

To My Daughter:

If possible in the years to come build on the legacy, teachings, and knowledge I have given you throughout these many years – If I am unable please try to build a lasting foundation for future generation to come – Be the Patriarch and use the KJV or NKJV Holy Bible as Your Guide.

Remember – Think to for Yourself & Learn Directly from God – Don't get caught up in churches or religion – Stick to the personal relationship with God you have and teach this to your family to come – I love You!

Forward

This book has been developed for my daughter who is currently 10. Looking forward as any good father does I felt the need to develop this book in the event I am not around to guide her through life as she ages and matures into the beautiful young lady of integrity I am sure through the Spirit of God she will blossom into.

With the world as crazy as it is right now – Massive rapes all arcos Europe from Muslims, Massive relocations of South Americans into the United States, Crime Out of Control everywhere, Governments pushing division . . . the world truly looks to have a dark future.

Nevertheless there is hope in God despite these things, despite all that we see or hear – for we walk by faith not be sight and we walk courageously in love standing up to all giants and not in fear.

If there is ever a time to "Take Action for the Kingdom of God" it is now – Plan accordingly my brothers and sisters for tomorrow is not guaranteed.

Chapter 1:
God's Standard

Sure, it's just a date right? It's nothing harmless. In fact, everybody is going out on a date — your friends, people at your school, every one you know have already went on a couple of dates. Yes, you're old enough to go out with someone, but what is your gut telling you? Are you being convicted by the Holy Spirit? Are you really ready to be dating?

Sam didn't know what to do. Tommy, who sat next to her in History and Math just asked her out on a date. Mary, Sam's best friend was ecstatic about the idea since she already started dating. In fact, she has already tried dating a couple of guys already; some of them were even their senior. But, Sam wasn't sure. She was also worried on how she will tell her parents that she will go out on a real date with a person of the opposite sex. Sam's parents aren't strict, in fact, they are actually supportive of her, and she has a close relationship with them. However, there was something at the back of Sam's mind making her feel uneasy of the idea of dating.

Growing up in a Christian family, Sam's parents taught her what the Bible said about courtship and dating. She knew that God has His own standards when it comes to these things. She knew that she should wait for God's timing when it comes to finding *the one*. But, what should Sam do? Tommy seemed to a nice guy to go out with and she didn't discern any bad intentions from him. Would she say "yes"? Or would she turn him down?

You might find yourself in the same situation as Sam. Maybe you've just reached the age when you feel like you're ready for dating, but still hesitant to try it. If you were in Sam's shoes, would you go out on a date with Tommy?

Maybe you're already in the age where almost everyone you know is starting to go out on dates. Like Sam, you might also have a best friend who is encouraging you to try dating, and sometimes you feel pressured to give in. But your parents aren't actually keen on the idea of you dating.

While you may feel that you don't totally understand your parents why they won't allow you to go on a date, if you carefully look at what the Bible says about being in a relationship with another person of the opposite sex, you will fully understand where your parents are coming from.

Chapter 2: Courtship

God's Standards for Courtship

God wants you to be another Christian like yourself

Being a Christian, you already know that you are part of God's family. You are His daughter that He cares so much about. Do you think a Father like Him will allow you to be with a man who is not part of His family? I guess not.

In 2 Corinthians 6:14, the apostle Paul wrote: *"Be ye not unequally yoked together with unbelievers: for what fellowship hath righteousness with unrighteousness? And what communion hath light with darkness?"*

Does this verse mean that you avoid making friends with unbelievers? Of course not! Paul's purpose for this is to remind the church at Corinth not to engage in partnership with unbelievers, because Christians and unbelievers are simply different from one another — different morals, beliefs, and faith.

But you're only going to get to know an unbeliever, right? You're not actually entering into a serious relationship yet. But, you must keep in mind that courting is actually an entry towards a lifetime of partnership — to marriage. What if you fell in love with this guy? Then you will become vulnerable. You don't want to come to a point where you have to abandon your Christian principles just to be with this guy. What if he wants you to "make love" with him, and yet you believe that you should save yourself until after marriage, can you hold your ground, even if he threatens to break up with you?

Do not allow yourself to go through such a heartache just because you chose someone who rejects God. Many who still pursue dating non-Christians believe that "This person will change." However, I have to remind you that only God can change people's heart. Yes, you can continually pray and ask God to change the person you care about, however, 2 Corinthians 6:14 doesn't tell us to not be equally yoked together…until a person changes. It is God's reminder for Christians not to partner with unbelievers!

Do you want to know what will happen if you allow yourself to be in partnership with people who reject God? **Read Deuteronomy 7:3-6.**

God Doesn't Want to be Number 2:

This is a biggie . . . Our God is a jealous God, as His name is Jealous (Exodus 34:14). Even your earthly father wouldn't want you to be too much into someone that you will forget about everything and everybody else; much more is our God.

Even if you're dating a Christian, it doesn't mean that God is OK with you placing Him in the back seat of your priorities. Even though you're so in love and you feel that the person you care about is someone you can't live without, your priority should only be Him alone. A pastor in one of his sermons once said, "God wants to be your first and only priority. Your career, wealth, love life, and everything else falls on a different category." God is a jealous God, and He doesn't want to share His spot in your life with nothing else.

Even before you start getting into courting and entering a serious relationship with another person, make sure that you have made it clear to him that he's only second to you and that God should always be #1.

Do you want to know whether a man is a real Christian? That is if he understands that your relationship with him is only going to be your second priority and that he too, has God as his #1 priority.

God wants You to Save Yourself for Marriage

Yes, dating will put you on a vulnerable spot, especially when you're engaged in a relationship with a non-believer. You see, the world has a different standard when it comes to dating. The media will tell you that it's normal to engage in sexual activities between dating individuals because it is how you show your affection to the other person.

While man was created by God to feel loved by skin-to-skin contact, but it doesn't mean that you should allow yourself to be physically involved when you're dating. Holding hands, hugging, and kissing, may seem usual and harmless, but this could lead to having sex. If you read what the Scripture says, you will clearly see that the Bible tells us that sex should only happen between two married couples and having intercourse out of marriage is clearly a sin. More than worrying about feeling worthless after giving up your virginity to another person and then just being left alone, or worrying about getting pregnant because you're already having sex, what you need to think about is God's judgement to people to those who disobeys Him.

Remember that you are precious in the eyes of your earthly father and your Father in heaven. They don't want you to get hurt, or worse, face the consequences of your poor choices. Guard yourself, use God's word as an armor to protect yourself from falling into the standards of this world. The Bible says in *Romans 12:22* *"And be not conformed to this world: be ye transformed by the renewing of your mind, that ye may prove what is that good, and acceptable, and perfect, will of God."*

God wants you to choose a quality man

Finally, as a daughter the King of Kings, of course, He wants His princess to find a quality man. Proverbs 31 talks about a noble woman's character, and in verse 23, it shows what a noble woman's husband should be: "Her husband is respected at the city gate, where he takes his seat among the elders of the land."

God wants you to choose a man who's not only respected in the community, but He wants you to be with someone who is also faithful to God. From this early on, pray that God will give you the discernment about the men who will come into your life. Choose the one that not only know God's Word, but also lives it—someone who understands why God should be the center of your relationship and how your partnership should bring honor and glory to God's name.

Chapter 3:
True Love Waits

Everybody says it's OK, but you know it's not. You might even be mocked by your friends for being a virgin, but you know it is the right thing to do. In a time where sex is nothing but a casual "activity" between individuals, staying a virgin until marriage seems like an impossible feat. But, let me tell you this: God is pleased when you save yourself until marriage because that's the exactly how he designed sex to be. Sex should only be between a married couple, Genesis 2:24 tells us *"Therefore shall a man leave his father and his mother, and shall cleave unto his wife: and they shall be one flesh."*

Unfortunately, the world has twisted the meaning of sex. Sex nowadays is something that people casually do. The hard truth is, some people have sex just for the sake of it, and not because they love each other. Some have sex with the same gender, and others, to multiple partners. The world's definition of sex is such a great defiance of God's beautiful gift to a husband and wife.

Chapter 4:
God's Purpose for Sex

Reproduction

This is quite one of the most
obvious purposes of sex between
married couples. After God had
created man, male and female
(Genesis 1:27), He then blessed
them and charged them with a
command, "...*Be fruitful and
multiply, and replenish the earth, and
subdue it: and have dominion over the
fish of the sea, and over the fowl of the
air, and over every living thing that
moveth upon the earth.*" In the
further chapters of the book of
Genesis, you can see God
instituting two holy institutions
which are *marriage* and *family*.

This again, obviously tells us that God's charge
for us to procreate should be within the holy
institution of marriage between a male and a

female, He wants children to be conceived and born in a family.

Expression of Love

Many actually abuse this, believing that sex is a way of expressing their affection for a person whom they love; even outside of marriage. Yet, we go back to our Biblical understanding that sex should only be between a married male and female. In Ephesians 5:25-31, Paul reminds us that the purpose of marriage and becoming one flesh (sex) is love.

"Husbands, love your wives, even as Christ also loved the church, and gave Himself for it...(v.28) So ought men to love their wives as their own bodies. He that loveth his wife loveth himself. For no man ever yet hated his own flesh; but nourisheth and cherisheth it, even as the Lord the church... (v.31) For this cause shall a man leave his father and mother, and shall be joined unto his wife, they two shall be one flesh."

Pleasure

This might surprise you, as you may feel that having pleasure in sex with your spouse is unbecoming of a Christian. But you have to understand that man is also designed by God to give pleasure and to receive pleasure as well. In fact, you can also see an entire book of the Bible (Song of Songs) that is about the sensual and romantic love that is shared between a man and a woman, and you can see in Song of Songs 2:10-13 about a man's invitation to a woman to be his partner in pleasure.

However, you have to keep in mind that pleasure in sex is only a part of a marriage. Being married together also means having pleasure with waking up beside each other every day, watching the sunset go down, and hearing your children's laughter. Yes, sex is also for pleasure, but it is only to be enjoyed by a man and a woman within their marriage.

Bounding

Another purpose for sex is for two individuals, husband and wife, to be bonded together as one. Remember, marriage is designed for two lives to be as one in serving and glorify God. And to be united with each other, couples should get to know each other in a deeper sense.

Genesis 4:1 tells us, *"…Adam knew Eve his wife; and she conceived, and bore Cain, and said, I have gotten a man from the Lord."* Of course, we know that the word *knew*, means Adam and Eve, being a married couple, had an intercourse and were blessed to have their first born. But a deeper understanding of this word tells us that Adam not only had sex with his wife, but he also got to bond with her, to get to know her deeply, physically, emotionally, and spiritually.

Chapter 5:
Waiting for Love

Now that we have laid God's true purpose for intercourse, I hope you fully understand how important saving yourself until marriage is so important, especially to God, our Father. The apostle Paul wrote in *1 Corinthians 6:18-19*, *"Flee from fornication. Every sin that a man doeth is without the body; but he that commmiteth fornication sinneth against his own body. What? Know ye not that your body is the temple of the Holy Ghost which is in you, which ye have of God, and ye are not your own? For ye are bought with a price: therefore glorify God in your body, and in your spirit, which are God's."*

The question now is, what then should you do now that you're still young and isn't ready for marriage yet?

Be Filled with God's Word

It's true that in this generation, falling into temptation is easier compared to decades ago. Today, as early as you hit puberty, you might notice your peers are already engaged in sexual activities, having sex is already a norm. Pornography isn't now only limited to Playboy magazines or adults films, now, you can see naked women on the internet, music videos, Miley Cyrus "twerking" and posing for photos wearing almost nothing, and you see mainstream movies and TV series with lots of sexy scenes.

The Scripture is full of warnings to help us avoid falling into sin and you can also see plenty of God's promises to those who avoid it. The Bible is our armor in order to fight temptation, Ephesians 6:11 says, *"Put on the whole armor of God, that ye may be able to stand against the wiles of the devil."*

When we fill our minds with God's Word, we have nothing else to focus on but His Word. *"But seek ye first the kingdom of God, and His righteousness; and all these things shall be added unto you." Matthew 6:33*

Surround Yourself with Believers of the Same Sex.

While there's nothing wrong with being friends with unbelievers, (In fact, this could be your opportunity to share the gospel!), but surrounding yourself with people who share the same faith, like the people in your church, will help you avoid temptation. Help each other to be deeper in your spiritual walk. Share your struggles and ask for prayers. It might also help if you seek guidance from mature Christians who will guide you and help you overcome what you're facing.

"He that walketh with wise men shall be wise: but a companion of fools shall be destroyed." Proverbs 13:20

Do Not Place Yourself in a Situation where You'll be Tempted

Even though you feel that you know how to stand your ground and is able to turn away from temptation when it comes, it would be better if you do not allow yourself to be close to the invitation to sin. Remember that the devil works double to make Christians fall into sin. Being alone with a date in your home may seem harmless, but this is definitely one example of you putting yourself in a situation where you will be tempted to fall into sin.

"Watch ye therefore, and pray always, that ye may be accounted worthy to escape all these things that shall come to pass, and to stand before the Son of man." Luke 21:36

Profess Your Beliefs

Even if you get rejected, and even if it means turning down the guys who would like to ask you on a date. God is pleased when you let other people know your commitment to sexual purity. People who won't respect this only means that they don't deserve to be a part of your life. Don't be afraid to commit to this and to stand firm on this, for this is what God wants you to do. Wait on true love, wait on the Lord, for He has promised good things to his children who obey.

"Therefore, my beloved brethren, be ye steadfast, unmovable, always bounding in the work of the Lord, forasmuch as ye know that your labor is not in vain in the Lord." 1 Corinthians 15:58

Chapter 6: Consequences of Sin

Like your earthly father, our God and Father in heaven is concerned about our well-being. He of course, wants to give you great things, but like your Dad, God will also allow you to face the consequences of your sin to remind you that you're disobeying Him and to also lead you again to His path.

Remember that our God has many names. He has been called a loving God, a gracious God, an all-knowing God, and He is also a just God. All throughout the Bible, we see God's calling for us to obey Him, and in it, we can also see the consequences of defying Him.

Many people today might not see pre-marital sex as a sin, but this is just like any other "grave" sins; and committing it has also consequences.

"Know ye not that the unrighteous shall not inherit the kingdom of God? Be not deceived: neither fornicators, nor idolaters, nor adulterers, nor effeminate, nor abusers of themselves with mankind, nor thieves, nor covetous, nor drunkards, nor revilers, nor extortioners, shall inherit the kingdom of God." 1 Corinthians 6:9-10

If you study the Bible real well, you'll see that there are a lot of verses that shows us the consequences of sin, but what exactly are they?

It Separates You From God

Isaiah 59:2a makes it clear for us that sins creates a separation between us and God. This explains why we seem distant to the Lord whenever we live in sin. That's why sometimes you'll find it hard to pray, or even go to church when you don't ask for forgiveness from your sins. But don't misunderstand this as God moving away from you when you sin. In fact, God's love covers us even if we're sinners. The only reason why we feel distant from God is because we're the ones that's moving away from Him when we sin.

Remember in Genesis 3, when Adam and Eve fell into sin? Wasn't God the one who looked for them (v.9) after they became afraid and hid from God (v.10)? No, it doesn't mean that God didn't know where they were, but it only shows us that we are the ones who distances ourselves to God when we sin.

It Brings Destruction to Your Life

Another story from the book of Genesis is found in Chapter 19 where the Lord destroyed the cities of Sodom and Gomorrah. The men in the city were so into sin that God allowed wrath to happen in the city (v.13). The Lord rained down fire and sulfur from the sky to the both cities leaving everything in them to burn to the ground. The story of Noah, also in the book of Genesis (Chapters 6-7), is another example of God allowing destruction (Gen.6:17) through a great flood to wash out the wicked people.

You see, God might not be sending sulfur to rain down or a great flood, in our time, but this only shows us that we can face destruction whenever we sin and fail to ask God's forgiveness for it.

It Hurts Others

Don't ever think that sinning only affects you. In fact, sinning also hurts that people who loves you and cares for you.

One pastor's daughter in a local church admitted to her parents that she was pregnant out of wedlock. Of course, this hurt her father a lot. Being a minister, seeing your child fall into sin is like a direct stab to the heart. Of course, God's forgiveness is always there, but this situation not only hurts the parents, but it can also lead some of the congregation to stumble.

Imagine, if you allow yourself to engage in sexual activity, don't you think you're hurting the people you love because you are putting yourself on dangerous grounds?

It Leads You to Sin More

Any sin that you repeatedly commit and fail to repent to God leads you to more sin. A "simple" kiss, leads to petting, caressing, and then finally leads to having sex. What seemed harmless in the beginning ended up you finding yourself in deep waters with no way out.

Unless you listen to the Holy Spirit convicting you, and repent to God your sins, you will see yourself committing sin, after sin, after sin.

"Repent ye therefore, and be converted, that your sins may be blotted out, when the times of refreshing shall come from the presence of the Lord;" Acts 3:19

It Sentences You to Eternal Damnation

Romans 6:13 is clear, to tell us that *"...the wages of sin is death;"* If you're a believer and know what God wants us to do, but disobeys Him, you also commit sin (James 4:17).

My prayer is that as a Christian, you won't allow your sins to be unforgiven by God. Yes, it is in our nature to sin, that's why God has allowed Jesus to die on the cross for our sins and in our stead. It is you and I who deserves death because we are sinners, but Christ became the perfect lamb, the sacrifice to wash us from our sins; and I hope that you won't forget that. God's forgiveness is always available; you just have to ask for it.

Chapter 7:
Dad's Expectations

Just like your Father in Heaven, your Dad cares a lot about you. Sometimes you may feel that your parents hate you because they're being too overprotective and that they're not letting experience "the good things". As your parents, this is their way of showing you how much they love you and care for you. When you become a parent you will understand how your folks feel; how they will do everything to protect you and to make sure that you won't get hurt. And believe it or not, even if you're already an adult, your parents will always see you as their little one—the baby always need their guidance and help. So don't take it against them if they don't allow you to go out on dates or feel that you're still too young for courtship.

Exodus 20:12 tells us to *"Honor thy father and thy mother: that thy days may be long upon the land which the Lord thy God giveth thee."* This commandment won't be given by our Lord if children are better than their parents. The Lord has instructed this because He knows that parents will do everything to guide their children into the right path; including helping their child find the perfect partner in life.

Now the question is, just what exactly are your Dad's standard to courtship are?

You can only enter into Courtship when You're Mature enough

I have to say this, but it is really hard for parents to admit that their child is old or mature enough to enter into courtship, however this is inevitable. Of course, as parents, we want to see our little baby to also grow up as a mature adult and end up with the right man. However, you should definitely wait until your parents allow you to go into the process of courting. Your parents know best when you are mentally, emotionally, and physically mature enough to get into a deeper relationship with another person; so you really have to respect your parents when they tell you that you can't date or go into courting yet.

You need to ask for Approval First

All parents want to be with you every step of the way, that's why it means to them when you seek their approval first before going through the process of courting. Of course, this means that if a man wants to pursue you, he must first ask your parent's permission to officially court you.

Don't look at this as a hindrance for you to finding a right man for you. This is you showing your parents how much you respect them by asking their permission. This is also your chance to see if the man who wants to pursue you is really serious in getting to know you better by meeting your parents and seeking their approval for courtship.

We want someone who loves God above All else.

Any many who is an unbeliever has no business in courting our daughter; and I believe this is what your parents' standard is too.

"Neither shalt thou make marriages with them; thy daughter though shalt not give unto his son, nor his daughter shalt thou take unto thy son. For they may serve other gods: so will the anger of the Lord be kindled against you, and destroy thee suddenly." Deuteronomy 7:3-4

Of course, your folks want you to be with someone who loves God above else, and someone who will bring you closer to Him and not away from Him. We all know that any relationship doesn't have Christ as the center of it is weak; and as parents, we don't want to see you go through heartaches as a consequences of being involved with an unbeliever.

We want someone who Respects You

Of course, every parent wants this for their daughter. That's why it's important for parents to meet the guy who wants to pursue you first because this shows that he has high respect for you and your parents. Even before you enter into courtship, let the guy know about your boundaries — that you don't believe in physical contact, that you're saving yourself from marriage, and that you have to get to know each other deeply.

Go out on Group Dates

Even if your parents already allowed you to enter into the courting process, it doesn't mean that it's OK for you to go out on a date alone with your suitor. Like I said in the previous chapter, do not allow yourself to be in a place where you'll be tempted. Going to the movies alone with your suitor can lead you into temptation. If your suitor wants to go out with you, he must know that your dates should be chaperoned or be with a group. It doesn't have to be with your parents all the time, you could go out with the other younger couples from your church, or the other members of the family like your brothers or sisters.

Don't look at this as something that might hinder you from getting to know the person a little bit deeper. Take this as an opportunity to see how your suitor gets along with the other people in your life.

We want you to marry a quality man

Just like God, your earthly parents also wants you to end up with a quality man — someone who has the right concept of family, someone who has aspirations on their education and career, someone who is a good provider and can handle money well, and most importantly, someone who is a believer and practices his faith.

This is why the process of courtship is so important because you can get to know a person not only on their physical attractiveness, but you can also discover something deeper about them, about their spirituality, about their beliefs and about their dreams and aspirations.

Your parents' standards might seem irrational, but if you try to understand them a little more, you will see that their courtship rules are not for them, but for your benefit. Any man who is willing to work within the boundaries you set and who is willing to honor your parents' rules is definitely someone who is worthy of you.

Chapter 8: You Are The Treasure

You are special. No matter how many people tell you that you are not and no matter how many flaws that you have, in God's eyes (and in your parents' eyes), you are special. Like I said a couple of times earlier, as a believer of Christ you have become a part of God's family (Galatians 3:26). This means that you are a princess because you are the daughter of the Kings of Kings, so don't allow yourself to be any lesser than that.

The world tells us that it's OK to go out and make yourself available to men, but you have to know that you are more precious than that. Keep in mind, that **you are the treasure so don't go out looking for love — you have to allow the treasure hunters to look for you.** God's will for you is to find someone whom you will end up marrying (1 Corinthians 7:1-3). He didn't want you to go out on several dates with different men to find the one that's perfect for you, He wants you to patiently wait for His timing and to allow His will to unfold in your life.

Psalm 37:4 tells us to *"Delight thyself also in the Lord: and He shall give thee the desires of thine heart"* This means that when we find delight in serving God, reading His Word, and following His commands, He will bless us with what we're praying for according to His will. In this context, He will lead you to the man He created perfectly for you. You don't have to make yourself available and be in a treasure hunt to look for the right man, God wants you be and treasure and He wants you to wait.

Now, this may seem exasperating to you, especially if you see your friends and everyone around you already being involved in a serious relationship with another person. But let me tell you this, waiting for God's perfect timing means that He is preparing you for something great. *"How precious also are thy thoughts unto me, O God! How great is the sum of them!"* Psalm 139-17

When you start to become frustrated waiting for God to give you the "perfect one", allow yourself to remember these things:

God has a Great Plan for Your Life

His will may not fall well with yours, but remember that His plan is always the best. Even before you were born, God already knows everything about you (Psalm 139), He knows what you need, and He has your best interest in mind.

In Jeremiah 29:11 God promised the nation of Israel of His great plans. Although this promise wasn't directed on us, we can use this verse to remind us that our God who never changes, also has great plans for you and me!

God is Preparing You for Greater Things

Don't ever think that there's nothing happening when you're waiting. In fact, when you wait on God, you start to be anxious on something, so that when His time comes and answer your prayer, you become to appreciate more what He has given you.

God is building Your Patience

Praying and waiting on God builds your patience not only to wait on the perfect man for you, but He is also preparing you to wait for bigger things that He has to offer you.

"Wait on the Lord: be of good courage, and He shall strengthen thine hear: wait, I say, on the Lord." Psalm 27:14

God is Transforming Your Character

By waiting on God's timing and trusting His will, you are allowing the Lord also transform you completely so that you will be ready when the one you're praying for comes in your life.

"Knowing this, that the trying of your faith worketh patience. But let patience have her perfect work, that ye may be perfect and entire, wanting nothing." James 1:3-4

God is Teaching You to Trust Only Him

Finally, praying and waiting on the Lord for the man you will marry also teaches you to trust God alone. You don't have to put yourself out there, because you know the He will make a way for you to end up with the man He just created for you.

Don't be too anxious when praying for the right man to come, if it's according to God's will, then he will surely come. Do not allow yourself to be pressured with the people surrounding you. Fill your mind with God's word and delight on His promises, surely God will grant you the desires of your heart.

Chapter 9:
You Set The Standard

Even before your parents allow you to enter into
the process of courtship, there might be several
guys who will show interest on you. However, it
is up to you whether you reject or accept the
advances of these men. But like I said, if you're a
Christian, you must know that dating several
men, for the sake of having a special someone in
your life, or satisfying your physical needs,
without the intent of ending up in marriage is
not God's way.

Your Father in heaven, and your Dad here on
earth doesn't want you to be in a relationship
that will hurt you, that's why your parents
would want you to enter into a process of
courtship when you're mature enough. So you
don't have to go around and test the waters first
(dating) before you can say that you're ready for
marriage.

As we all know, the Bible clearly instructs us not
be equally yoked with unbelievers, but what else
do you need to look for in your future husband?
What do you need to pray for when asking God
for the right man to come in your life in the
future?

Here are some standards that you might want to keep when you're ready to go into courtship:

My future husband should be a servant of God

> How a guy looks, how fit he is, and how he carries his clothes should be the least of your concerns when setting the standards for the ideal man for you. More than his physical features, one of the top most criteria that you should pray for is that your future husband should be a servant of the Lord. Several verses in the Bible tell us that we should serve God, and also serve others as an act of worshipping the Lord, and this is one thing that you should look for in your future partner in life.

> When a man wants to court you, look at where he spends his time most. Does he serve in the church? Is he involved in a ministry? Does he find joy in serving others?

My future husband has respect for me

Another criteria that you may want to consider is looking for a guy who respects you (but then again, why are you looking for a guy? Remember you are the treasure not the treasure hunter). Even if you don't tell him about your vow of saving yourself until marriage, he will be the one who will take the initiative to respect your boundaries. There's no need for you to argue with him that you don't want physical contact during the process of courtship because he respects you and cares too much about you. Your future husband must love you like he loves himself (Ephesians 5:28-29).

My future husband has eyes only for me

As soon as you start getting to know another man, you will already know whether he is serious about pursuing you when he keeps his eyes only for you. Even if sexier girls, or women who you feel are better looking than you pass by, he won't allow himself to let his eyes wander, because he respects you. He will also avoid situations that will put him closer to temptation, not only because he loves you, but he is willing to follow God's command (Proverbs 4:23-25).

My future husband has goals and is ambitions for serving God

You know that a man will be a perfect husband and head of your household when he has ambitions and is actively seeking God's plan for his life. When you're married, you are to submit (Ephesians 5:22-23) yourself to your husband, that's why you want to look out for a man who knows how to steer his life through God's guidance.

My future husband glorifies God

It will be so easy for men to brag about their accomplishments when they don't have Christ in their lives. Of course, you don't want to be with someone who focuses on himself rather than caring for you and for others. You want your future husband to be good and yet, self-less. Find a mind that acknowledges that his accomplishments, his talents, and everything that is in his life comes from God. That it is the Lord that enables him to do such things.

My future husband love God above all else

This might be hard to understand for non-believers, but as Christians, you should want a man who loves God above you and everything else. This type of man will treat you far better than a guy who is just focused on loving you. This man willfully follows God's commands, will serve you, will love you, will be faithful for you and will give himself for you just as Jesus did for us and just as God has commanded.

These standards might seem an impossible feat, but remember that God only wants the best for you. He wants you to date a guy who will not only pass your standards, but pass His standards as well because He wants you to have a healthy and loving relationship—a type of relationship that can stand as a testimony to others and will bring back all the glory to His name.

Chapter 10:
Respect Yourself

Maybe at a young age you've already encountered people who made you feel that you are no better. Or maybe you're too focused on your flaws that's why often times you feel bad about yourself. Because of this, you either try your hardest to win other people's approval or you sulk and hate yourself because you're not that thin, your teeth are crooked, and you're not that physically attractive. But let me tell you this, even if other people make you feel bad, or even if you have tons of flaws, God still loves you!

If you're familiar with the story of creation in the book of Genesis, after God has created day and night, the heavens, the land and waters, the plants and the animals, He created man. And no, He didn't just create man out of nothing, He created man in His own image and likeness, *"So God created man in His own image; in the image of God He created Him; male and female He created them." Genesis 1:27;* this means, you are special! If you read God's word, you will see that there a lot of verses that tell you how important you are to God's eyes. One verse that reminds us about this is *Deuteronomy 7:6* that says, *"For thou art an holy people unto the Lord thy God: the Lord thy God hath chosen thee to be a special people unto Himself, above all people that are upon the face of the earth."*

But how come a lot of people try to change their appearance, which was made in God's image and likeness?

Maybe because they want to fit in, they want to impress the people they like, and gain more attraction. However, I'd have to tell you that you will not find true happiness when you focus on these things. It is only when you focus on God's love for you and accept Jesus Christ as your savoir will you find true joy. This is the joy that goes beyond your physical flaws and the joy that makes you love yourself and embrace the gifts that God has given you.

Now, when I say "self-love" I don't mean the conceited, self-centered love. What I'm talking about is the self-love that focuses on being thankful for what God has made and what He has blessed you with.

If you want to earn respect from other people, and probably attract a person you're interested in, then you must also start loving and respecting yourself even more. Stop changing yourself just so you can fit in to what most people as someone who is "beautiful" or "attractive". God uniquely designed each of us with spiritual gifts (1 Corinthians 12:1-11), and we are to use them to bring back honor and glory to our God. When we embrace these gifts, we allow ourselves to directly follow God's will in our lives, and through it we will be immensely blessed.

If you've been feeling lowly about yourself because of other people's mockery, or you have been hating yourself because you questioned your physical attractiveness, what you need to do is to start forgiving others and forgiving yourself as well. Don't allow the bondage of bitterness, rejection, and self-hatred hinder you from seeing the beauty of what God has blessed you with.

The Lord gave us a commandment to love others as we love ourselves (Mark 12:31) and it would be impossible to do that if you don't respect and love yourself first. Instead of wallowing in self-pity and wishing you were more attractive and beautiful, focus on praising God because He made you. *"I will praise thee; for I am fearfully and wonderfully made: marvelous are thy works; and that my soul knoweth right well." Psalm 139:14*

Chapter 11: Temptations

It's quite wrong to think that when you become a Christian, you will be immune from facing temptations. Do you think the devil is lurking around unbelievers? Of course not! They are already of this world and disobeying God has already been part of their daily lives. Satan's schemes is in fact focused on Christians; to see them stumble and fall into sin.

In Matthew 4:1-11, we can see the story of Jesus being tempted by the devil in the wilderness. After forty days and forty nights of prayer and fasting the devil dared to tempt Jesus not once, but three times in exchange for all "good things" that the devil has promised Christ. But how did our Lord Jesus respond to these temptations? He responded to the devil by saying that "man shall not live on bread alone," but on God's word, that the Lord should not be put into the test, and that man should only "worship the Lord your God, and serve Him only."

Maybe you've already experienced to be tempted in the past. In our time when our culture has been highly sexualized and having intercourse out of marriage has become a norm, it's quite difficult not to fall into sin and to keep yourself pure until your marriage. You see, it's actually normal to feel tempted about these things, however, it is how you respond to them that actually counts. Jesus was also tempted by the devil, but his response to it that made the difference.

The Bible also reminds us to be vigilant against falling into temptation: *"Be sober, be vigilant; because your adversary the devil, as a roaring lion, walketh about, seeking whom he may devour"* 1 Peter 5:8. That's why even before temptation would come your way, it would be wise if you have already shielded yourself from sin.

Move Your Focus Away from Sexuality

It's true that man and woman were created as sexual beings. In fact, one of the first commands of God to man is to *"be fruitful and multiply, and replenish the earth, and subdue it;"* That's why it will be inevitable for humans not to be sexually attracted to another person. But, you also have to remind yourself that this command from God was made only for a married man and woman.

You may encounter some situations where you will become sexually attracted to a guy, but you must learn to turn away from this desire, even if it's difficult. Dr. Jessica McCleese, an expert of Christian sex therapy says that one way to do this is to acknowledge that our sexual nature is only a small part of who we are; God made us with so many more things! "When our sexual selves are the focus, we lose who we are as whole people. If we can learn to see ourselves body, soul, and spirit, it becomes easier to save your whole self for marriage, says Dr. McCleese in a published interview online.

Don't be afraid to discuss your boundaries

When you enter into the process of courtship with another man, it would be right if you discuss with one another the physical boundaries that you two have. Be bold when you share your "rules" on courtship, and when you go out on dates, or do activities together, it would be better if you do it with a group. *Timothy 2:22* says, *"Flee also youthful lusts: but follow righteousness, faith, charity, peace, with them that call on the Lord out of a pure heart"* and setting boundaries and sticking with them would help you do this.

Find a person you can trust (God?)

Temptation can have a strong hold in you if you try to battle it on your own. However, it will become weak if you share your struggles with another person, like a mentor or an "accountability partner". Find a person whom your trust (another female), and most importantly, a Christian who can give you good advice and can help you pray to get over the temptations you are facing. However, God is the Best Option as people will always let you down in some way.

Allow the Holy Spirit to Lead & Guide You

Pray and always ask the Holy Spirit to lead you. Even if you're already entered into courtship, as individuals and as a couple, you should continually seek God's guidance and immerse yourself into the scripture—these things are your best defense against temptation. Galatians 5:16 tells us that we are able to turn away from our sinful nature when we walk in the Spirit. We are able to focus on things that are honest, just, pure, and lovely (Philippians 4:8).

Chapter 12:
What If I Stumble?

Maybe you feel that it's too late. Maybe you've already fallen into sin, is there still a way out?

I remember one song in the 90's by a Christian rock and rap group DC Talk "What if I Stumble?" and there's one phrase in the lyrics that truly struck me, it was "I hear you whispering my name 'My love for you will never change.'" This is a great reminder for all of us that even if we fall, even if we are sinners, God's love for us will never change.

"It is of the Lord's mercies that we are not consumed, because His compassions fail not." Lamentations 3:22

The Forgiving Father

The parable of the Prodigal Son (Luke 15:11-32) is a story of a man who had two sons. The younger son asked his father to give him the share of his wealth even before his father dies. Of course, we all know that the younger son squandered all his money living the life he wanted, until he ran out of money and began to starve. He was so hungry that even the pods that were given to the pigs looked appetizing to him. This is when he finally came to his senses that he should go home to his father and seek his forgiveness; and so he returned home.

However, even he was still a long way off from his home, his father already saw him and ran to him to embrace and kiss his son. His father even instructed his servants to dress him with the finest robe, place a ring on his finger and sandals under his feet. He even commanded to kill the fattened calf and celebrate with a feast. The older brother on the other hand was angry because his father was celebrating the homecoming of his brother who did nothing but waste his father's money, while he was always faithful in serving his father.

However, his father with this, *"...Son, thou art ever with me, and all that I have is thine. It was meet that we should make merry, and be glad: for this thy brother was dead, and is alive again, and was lost, and is found."*

Most people who would come across this parable would focus on the prodigal son's story of repentance, how he admitted his wrongdoings and asked his father's forgiveness.

However, what other miss is the real highlight of this story, which was the prodigal son's forgiving father. Notice that the father ran to embrace and kiss his son even before the younger son reached their home? If you were in the father's shoes, and your child has asked for his inheritance even before you were dead and then squandered it, would you welcome him back with open arms and throw a feast for him? I bet not. But the forgiving father is a great illustration of how our Father in heaven is.

Our Lord loves us so much that He is more than willing to forgive us and throw a "feast" for us when we repent and ask for his forgiveness.

"I, even I, am He that blotteth out thy transgressions for Mine own sake, and will not remember thy sins."
Isaiah 43:25

But of course, we don't use the Lord's forgiveness as our license to freely commit sin. For the Lord hates sin. However, what He wants us to do when we stumble is to confess our sins before our God, ask for restoration, and repent.

"..If thou return, then will I bring thee again, and thou shalt stand before me..." Jeremiah 15:19

If you commit sin, you may have to endure the consequences of your actions because our God is a just God. However, if you turn away from sin and ask the Lord for forgiveness and attempt to honor Him with your life, God will surely pour out His blessings upon you.

What are the sins that you need to confess to the Lord? Pray and ask for His forgiveness!

Chapter 13:
God's Blessings

A Personal Story from a Friend:

My name is Gabrielle, and this is my testimony.

I don't have a tragic story to tell that will bring everybody to tears. In fact, my story might seem ordinary compared to yours, but out of this "plain" story is God's extraordinary blessings pouring out, and I couldn't just sit back and not let everyone know about it.

I grew up in a Christian home. When I was young, I would attend Sunday school every week. There, I learned stories of the "heroes" in the Bible. I learned about Noah and his obedience to God, Moses and the Israelites' exodus from Egypt to the Promised Land, the consequence of Jonah's disobedience to God's command, Jesus' parables and many more. My mom taught me how to pray, and I would always do this before eating, and before going to bed.

However, as I grew older, going to church and praying only became a routine for me.

When I was 14 years old, an evangelist from our church visited our home once. For an hour, she explained to me how I needed repent and accept Jesus as my personal Lord and Savior. I couldn't forget that day. That's because even though I have been attending church all my life, it was only then that I understood what salvation really meant. I prayed the sinner's prayer that day and received God's gift of salvation. From then on, I became active in our church. I was involved in several ministries and was able disciple a couple of younger kids attending our church. Then came my senior year in high school.

I met a young man who wished to pursue me and date me. Being surrounded with friends that were already in relationships, I allowed him to court me without the permission of my parents. My mind was telling me that there's nothing wrong about this since I wasn't jumping into a serious relationship, and I didn't have plans to elope with him in the near future. However, my heart was telling me that I made a wrong decision. Not only because I didn't ask my parents' permission first, but most importantly, because he wasn't a believer.

Being a guy who knows how to swoon me, it didn't take long until we finally called ourselves boyfriend-girlfriend before we graduated high school. We went out on dates, spent the most of the time we had with each other before we parted ways because we will be going to different colleges the following school year.

I always prayed to God that I could win him over when I shared the gospel to him. When I had the opportunity, he listened to what I said, but told me that he wasn't ready to become "religious". Because I was already in love with this guy (or at least I thought I was), I didn't see this as a red flag; I was too blindly in love with him.

However, after several months I noticed that we were starting to become more physical. During the early stages of our relationship, all we did was hold hands, and then he started to hug me, and then kiss me on the cheeks. One time, he tried to kiss me on the lips. I knew in my heart that it was wrong, but I allowed it to happen because I thought I was in love. Then came the time that he was already giving me hints that we should "do it". One time, he tried to invite me to his house, only to find out that we were the only ones who will be there.

This was my wake up call. Even though it was hard for me, and it broke my heart, I had to call it quits with him. God made me realized that I was already conforming to the patterns of this world, and that I was playing with fire for too long.

Although I had to endure the pain of letting someone I love go (sleepless nights and endless crying) and although he didn't seem to fully understand my reasons why I was breaking up with him, I felt blessed because God made a way for me to move out of a relationship that would cause me to sin and break my vow to be pure until marriage.

From then on, I focused on my ministry and my studies. Jaci Velasquez' "I Promise" became my favorite song. The lyrics "So I promise to be true to You. To live my life in purity as unto You. Waiting for the day, when I hear You say, here is the one I have created just for you," was written in my heart.

Then my sophomore year in college came. I became very active in one of the organizations in our campus. I was friends with everyone except for this one guy, Matt, whom I didn't seem to notice at all. Funny thing is, after we were formally introduced to each other, we became inseparable. We became friends, talked and texted almost all the time, and shared stories about all things under the sun. The great thing about him is that he was a believer just like me. In our conversations, we would share about our faith and our experiences in serving God's ministry. And then, the inevitable happened. One day, we both realized that we were starting to like each other, more than just friends.

Coming out of a failed relationship, I knew I had to do it right this time. Matt knew that I believed in courtship so he took the initiative to come to our house and meet my parents. This was his way of asking them that he wanted to court me. He made clear to my parents of his intentions and my parents didn't have any problems with this. Knowing that he was a true Christian was enough for them to know that he respects me and is serious about pursuing me.

Of course, Matt and I went out on dates. We enjoyed doing things together like having coffee, walking our dogs to the park, and other things activities that couples do. We also tried attending the same church, served the Lord through the music ministry, and would even share the verses we read during our personal quiet time. Even if we considered ourselves as a couple, we both made sure that we won't be in a situation where we will tested to do things that wouldn't please God.

In college having sex when you are in a relationship (or even when you're not) was normal. In fact, everyone we knew had active sex lives. My friends from college who had boyfriends were doing "doing it" like it was no big deal. But, I was blessed that Matt too believed that we should wait until marriage.

No, it wasn't easy for us to remain pure. We were obviously attracted to each other, and there were times that we were tempted to give in, but our prayers and our faith helped us a lot. We would often be teased that we were the only virgin couple in campus, but we didn't care. All we cared about was doing what was pleasing to God's eyes.

It took amazing seven years before Matt proposed for marriage. What impressed me most about him is that he asked my parents' blessing first (without me knowing) before he even asked me to marry him. I would often tease him that he was too confident that I would say "yes" to him. Of course, my parents gave their blessing and of course, I said "yes".

Planning for our wedding wasn't easy because we decided that as a couple, we will be the ones to shoulder the expenses for it. We knew what we wanted for our dream wedding, but it seemed like we didn't have enough resources to pull it off. We were just starting off with our careers and just had meager savings to pay for a grand wedding. This is when we truly felt God's hand working to make our dream wedding come true. Without even asking, the people close to us would volunteer to pay for some of the costs for our wedding, one even paid for our reception, which was the bulk of our expenses! And I couldn't simply put into words how our wedding turned out to be, the experience was just unforgettable! Almost everyone who attended our wedding were in tears when we exchanged our vows. Our guests said that they truly felt how in love we were and how happy we were to be married; they felt that our marriage was truly blessed by God!

Looking back, I realized that our dream wedding coming to life was only a sample of what God has prepared for us. Our wedding day was only the surface of one of the best blessing that our Lord has set especially for us — and that was our marriage. Every single day, I would thank God for the chance of waking up beside someone I love. I had the opportunity to serve the Lord with my partner in life. More than having the chance to be physically intimate with my husband, I thank the Lord because He has given me someone whom I can confide with, someone whom I can fight my battles with, and someone whom I can build my dreams with. "I found the one whom my soul loves."

No, Matt and I are not a perfect couple. There are times that we argue even on petty little things, but at the end of the day it is our love for God and love for each other that makes our journey together even more awesome.

I thank the Lord because He gave me a chance to get out of a wrong relationship before it was too late. I thank God because He blessed me with a man He created especially for me. I thank Him because He gave me a man who loved me and respected me. I thank the Lord because he gave us the strength to turn away from temptation and not fall into sin. I thank Him for this because my husband and I can testify that *it is possible to remain pure until marriage* through the help of God.

My prayer for you is that you remain vigilant and continually seek the Holy Spirit's guidance to help you get through temptation. Yes, it is hard to remain pure until marriage, but we have to claim the Lord's promise in Galatians 6:9 that <u>those who do not faint shall reap a harvest of blessing in God's perfect time.</u>

My story won't hit the box office if it were made into a film, but it's a simple testimony on how God is faithful to those who remain faithful to Him. The Lord has promised immense blessings to those who obeys His will, and I've seen it firsthand; He has given me and my husband the great gift of marriage.

Chapter 14: Conclusion

A lot has been written in such a small book, but important words nonetheless, simple easy to understand words that can help guide you along life's ups and downs if for whatever reason I'm not around.

Follow the principles in the Word of God, use this books as a quick reference, but understand the closer you get to God the more the enemy will attack you with temptation – so be ready for it. Remember we are in a Spiritual War and You need to take that seriously. What you bind in heaven through prayer will be bound here on earth in the Spiritual realm. This book is about relationships, courtship, dating etc. but at the same time it is really about helping you prepare for the Spiritual Warfare that will soon come by understanding the expectations of your Heavenly Father and your earthly father.

The devil tries so hard to use this time in your life to get you off track so you won't be blessed by God – Don't let the devil steel your future. Trust in God, Follow His Word, Be True to Yourself and Live with No Regrets unto God – But the secret to doing that is Knowing Yourself and Knowing who God is through His Word.

Remember what I used to say: Times Almost Up – Good Luck Buddy (a message to the devil). Yet rejoice not in that you have power over him and his workers but rather rejoice that Your Name is Written in the Lamb's Book of Life!

Referencces

http://www.ucg.org/bible-study-tools/booklets/marriage-and-family-the-missing-dimension/dating-dos-and-donts

http://www1.cbn.com/singles/dating-god-best-or-all-the-rest

http://www.gotquestions.org/dating-courting.html

http://www.middletownbiblechurch.org/prelatio/prelat8.htm

http://www.bible.ca/s-premarital-sex.htm

http://www.courageouschristianfather.com/true-love-waits/#axzz3x1mJsofV

http://www.ucg.org/vertical-thought/saving-sex-for-marriage-what-does-god-want-us-to-do

http://www.ucg.org/the-good-news/gods-purpose-for-sex-and-marriage

http://biblicalgenderroles.com/2015/02/10/the-7-reasons-why-god-made-sex/

http://www.crosswalk.com/family/singles/is-there-more-to-sex-than-pleasure-11572845.html

http://www.whatchristianswanttoknow.com/5-biblical-consequences-of-sin/

http://www.charismamag.com/life/men/22803-a-practical-and-biblical-understanding-of-dating-and-courtship

http://www.people.com/article/duggar-quotes-on-love-relationships-jessa-engaged-marriage-jill-michelle-jim-bob

http://www.relevantmagazine.com/god/practical-faith/5-reasons-god-makes-us-wait

https://unlockingfemininity.wordpress.com/2011/10/06/10-ways-to-know-if-hes-a-keeper/

http://biblereasons.com/loving-yourself/

http://www.greatbiblestudy.com/loving_yourself.php

http://www.boundless.org/relationships/2012/sex-series-waiting-while-dating

http://www.projectinspired.com/girl-to-girl-talk-how-to-avoid-temptation-and-wait-on-god/

http://www.christiananswers.net/q-dml/dml-y004.html

Special Gift

God has a Gift for You!

Plan of Salvation:

There is no formal " prayer of salvation" as many churches would have you believe, God's word is very clear – there is only one way to get to the Father in heaven and that is through Jesus Christ (John 14:6). Jesus says that you must be born again to enter into heaven (John 3:3-5).

Salvation is simply the first step in building an open & honest relationship with God. We all have sinned and fall short every day, but there is Hope in Jesus Christ – Just cry out to God in sincerity and honesty for forgiveness asking Him to Save you, Sanctify you, and fill you with His Holy Spirit – Ask for His will to be done in your life on earth as it is in Heaven – That's it, now just keep it real with God.

A Warning:

The Christian walk is not an easy life on the surface. The word of God says that we will be hated in all the world for Christ namesake (Matt. 24:9). The Bible says that in the last days are enemy prevail against us until Christ returns to save us (Dan 7:21, 22). Furthermore, we must endure hardship as a good soldier of Jesus Christ (2 Tim 2:3) – yet we are never alone in this, God promises us that He will never leave us nor forsake us if we believe in him (Matt.28:20).

In everything we go through we have the peace & joy of God which surpasses all understanding (Philp. 4:6-8) The Bible declares, "For I consider the sufferings of this present time are not worthy to be compared with the glory which shall be revealed in us. (Rom 8:18). However, in all these things we are more than conquerors through Jesus Christ (Rom. 8:37)

All Our Books

Click the Link Below:

Check Out All The American Christian Defense Alliance, Inc. Books Here

Contact Information

Stay in Contact with the American Christian
Defense Alliance, Inc

Contactus@acdainc.org

Or

Email Us Though
Our Website At:
http://acdainc.org

Join Our Mailing List

We also Greatly Appreciate You Signing Up For Our Mailing List and Providing a Good Rating for This Book.

If You or Your Family have been touched by this book please let us know by dropping us a line through our website at http://acdainc.org

Thanks Again for Reading

God Bless!

www.ingramcontent.com/pod-product-compliance
Lightning Source LLC
Chambersburg PA
CBHW032027040426
42448CB00006B/742